The Story with Grammar

Using story-based activities to develop knowledge of how language works

Book 1 – Parts of Speech

PUBLISHING

GRAMMAR MACHINE

Marie Langley

Title: The Story with Grammar Book 1:
Parts of Speech

Author: Marie Langley

Editor: Tanya Tremewan

Book code: PB00063

ISBN: 978-1-908735-43-0

Published: 2012

Publisher: TTS Group Ltd

Park Lane Business Park
Kirkby-in-Ashfield
Notts, NG17 9GU
Tel: 0800 318 686
Fax: 0800 137 525

Websites: www.tts-shopping.com

The author: Marie Langley taught for 19 years in both primary and secondary schools. In particular she taught English and was head of an English department for 10 years, as well as being deputy head for seven years. Her experience in the arts includes producing, writing and directing school productions and writing short stories, poetry and non-fiction for publication. Having completed a masters degree in education, she now works from home, at the top of the South Island of New Zealand in beautiful Golden Bay, as a freelance writer and editor.

CONTENTS

INTRODUCTION

Grammar is a word that can spark an emotional reaction. People get uncomfortable about it for different reasons. Some see grammar as a difficult subject; they have a sneaking, guilty feeling that maybe they should know more about it although they may not be convinced that it is necessary ('I do okay without being a grammar expert, so why should I bother?'). On the flip side, others – grammar 'experts' or those who know enough to spot some mistakes – bemoan the lack of grammar skills out there. In general, they believe that grammar rules must be upheld and that breaking them is a sign of laziness and ill discipline. An emotional topic indeed!

Certainly grammar rules are important. They provide the framework on which language is constructed and the mechanics of how we communicate. Without some semblance of agreed grammar rules, we wouldn't be able to use language to communicate at all. It is useful to know about grammar rules so that we can express ourselves clearly and accurately, such as in:

- a formal letter (eg, to apply for a job)

- an assignment, exam or other activity that is going to be judged in some way.

Even in informal messages such as short emails or text messages to friends, when we can get away with ignoring a few of the rules, we cannot ignore **all** the rules as then nothing would make sense and we could not communicate.

The limits of grammar knowledge are determined by an individual's ability and interest. The first step to developing both ability and interest is to encourage students to feel more comfortable about grammar and about language use in general. Helping students to develop their grammar basics will encourage their confidence as competent communicators. They will know the 'right way' to write and say things and understand why that way is right. This will help them with all types of written and spoken language.

This book presents some grammar basics at a level appropriate for Years 5–6. An understanding of how to apply these concepts will provide the basic framework for structuring grammar knowledge. This framework can then be strengthened and made more complex as students develop. Other books in *The Story with Grammar* series (also published by Essential Resources) can help in this process.

How to use this resource book

The Story with Grammar – Book 1: Parts of speech contains a series of short original stories. Each story is followed by activities that use examples from the story to illustrate various parts of speech. These activities provide opportunities for students to develop their understanding of parts of speech and to use them in practice. Answers are provided at the back, offering an additional learning tool if you choose to give them to the students for self-correction.

Before each activity, information is presented to clarify the related skill or concept. You could photocopy this information as a standalone unit to use in other ways, such as to display on the wall in a larger format as a reminder to students, to paste into workbooks or folders for quick reference and/or to incorporate into an assessment check system to record which concepts each student has grasped.

In terms of curriculum coverage, the activities fit well with the English curriculum, and may be used in a variety of ways, as identified below.

1. To assist the development of higher order processes such as critical thinking and to encourage the exploration of language, give out copies of the story and the related activities to the students. You may read the story and work through the activities together. Alternatively, provide them as individual activities or as homework for more able students.

2. Use the stories for **Close reading** practice (see 'Extra activity suggestions' on the next page). Create some comprehension questions, based on each text, to suit the ability level of your students. Assess understanding through oral questions and answers, or in a written format.

3. Use the stories as starters for writing activities:

   - In regard to **Expressive writing**, students could express their thoughts or feelings about what they have read.

   - Devise some **Transactional writing** tasks that relate to the texts, such as letters to the editor or newspaper reports about issues or incidents similar to those in the story or poem that the students have just read.

   - In terms of **Poetic writing**, students could write their own story or poem on a similar topic or from a similar viewpoint to the text they have just read.

4. Use these original stories as a basis for activities that develop other forms of language:

   - Develop **Oral language** skills by holding class discussions about what the students have read, asking them to construct and deliver speeches or debates on similar topics, and turning the story into performance scripts.

   - Introduce activities requiring **Visual language** techniques such as designing posters, covers or cartoons to go with the text.

The raw material is here. Use it in whatever way is appropriate for your students and the context in which you teach.

Extra activity suggestions

Story title	Close reading	Expressive writing	Transactional writing	Poetic writing	Oral language	Visual language
			Curriculum-related activities			
What's in a name?	To check comprehension, make up questions regarding *who, what, when, where, why* and *how*.	What makes you feel bored? Why?	Class rules for appropriate behaviour	Story about Tom's talk with Mr Sharp	Acting out the talk between Mr Sharp and Tom	Cartoon of the story
The thing is …		Which fitness activity do you prefer? Why?	Report on general fitness	Turn story into a ballad poem	Speech about fitness	'Get Fit' poster
It's a he	Include open-ended as well as closed questions.	Stray cats – who should look after them?	Letter to the council about stray cats	Story from the cat's viewpoint	Turning story into radio play	Poster for missing pet
This magic place	Questions may be asked by teacher or by students (peer assessment).	Where is your favourite holiday spot? Describe.	Travel article about Roz's holiday	Sense poem about staying at the story place	Role play of phone call between Roz and Chris	Travel brochure for the place in the story
Action stations		What is the best way to get to school? Why?	Letter to the editor against driving to work	Story about a new transport method for Alfie	Speech – the benefits of walking or biking	Leaflet promoting less traffic
You did that?	Answers may be given in writing or orally.	Grandparents coming to stay – your thoughts	Advice on relating to grandparents	Kit's diary	Gran's oral history about her schooldays	Cover of Kit's project
In a panic		Your favourite piece of clothing	Report on jumble sale	Play script of story	Acting out play script of story	Poster for jumble sale
Playing to learn		What do you think of computer games?	Directions to play a computer game	Poem about playing a computer game	Debate: computer games are not a good thing	Cover of a computer game package

Ready grammar reference

This page provides a quick check to help identify parts of speech. You may find it useful to copy it (enlarged if needed) and display it in students' folders or books, on the classroom wall and/or maybe even pinned up somewhere in students' homes.

The basic building blocks of grammar are words. We have to put words in a certain order to make sense. When we talk about **parts of speech**, we are talking about the job that each word in a piece of spoken or written communication does to help convey a message and make sense.

Part of speech	Definition	Examples
Noun	A word that names a person, animal, place or thing	*Tom, boy, desk, chair, cat*
Proper noun	A specific name for someone or something, which has a capital letter	*Mum, Tom, Dad, Toyota, Hillview, Mrs Jackson*
Common noun	A more general name, which doesn't need a capital letter	*dream, bed, school, mother*
Concrete noun	A name for something you can see and touch	*bike, shoes, steps, helmet*
Abstract noun	A name for something you can't see or touch, such as an emotion	*fun, boredom, happiness*
Pronoun	A word that stands in for a noun to save repetition	*I, you, he, she, it, we, they*
Possessive pronoun	A pronoun that shows ownership or belonging	*my, your, her, his, its, our, their*
Adjective	A word that describes a noun or pronoun	*magic, huge, small, little, awesome, gnarly*
Verb	A doing word that tells us what happens, the action	*look, walk, cycle, pedal, like*
Adverb	A word that adds information to a verb, giving more detail about the action	*honestly, suddenly, loudly, softly, usually*
Preposition	A word that shows position and how things relate in time and space	*in, on, between, above, before, after, at*
Conjunction	A joining word that connects parts of sentences and links ideas	*and, but, when, yet, because*

1. WHAT'S IN A NAME?

One day Tom decided it was time for a change. He had come up with a way to make life more interesting – or so he thought at the time. And, yes, it did make things more interesting but, in the end, it made things quite difficult as well.

You see, Tom decided that he would give a new name to everything around him. It started with a dream in which he was travelling in a spaceship. When Tom woke up, he decided that his bed was not a bed but a spaceship. That caused a bit of confusion when his mum said, 'Have you made your bed, Tom?' and Tom replied, 'No, but I've made my spaceship.' Mum gave him a funny look when he said that.

As the morning went by, Tom got more and more into his new way of naming things. The family cat, Sunny, was renamed Rainy. Dad's Toyota car became a Realota. Tom's school became Seahear instead of Hillview. His class teacher was called Mrs Jackson, but Tom said, 'Good morning, Mrs Jilldaughter'. Tom should have realised then that maybe he was taking the name thing too far when Mrs Jackson made a tutting sound and gave him a disapproving look.

At first, Tom's classmates thought his new names for everything were quite funny. They laughed when he called the desks chairs and the chairs desks. They thought it was especially funny when he climbed up on his desk after Mrs Jackson said, 'Sit down on your chairs, please'. She gave Tom a look even more loaded with disapproval than her earlier glare. He didn't notice – he was too busy thinking of new names for the windows and the door, and for the headmaster, Mr Sharp, who had just walked into the classroom.

That was when Tom really did go a bit too far. He said, 'Bad evening, Mr Blunt. I'm sitting on my chair as Mrs Jilldaughter asked us to do. Everyone else is sitting on their desks. Are you having a good night?'

There was a nervous giggle from one of the girls in the class but otherwise everything went very quiet. The silence was broken by Mr Sharp when he gave a small cough. Then he said, 'Mrs Jackson, I think Tom should come along to my office for a little chat about sensible behaviour.'

That's when Tom knew that 'interesting' could quickly become quite 'difficult'.

Work on your ... common nouns and proper nouns

Two major categories for nouns are **common** and **proper** nouns. But before we look at them, let's revise what nouns are.

A. Which word is a noun?

Here are some reminders about nouns:

- A noun is a word that names a person, place or thing.

- To find out if a word is a noun, try to put *the* in front of it. If the word makes sense when it is paired up in this way (eg, *the bed*), it is a noun. If it does not make sense (eg, *the decided*), it is usually a different part of speech.

---

1 Try putting *the* in front of each of the following words from the story. Tick it if you think it is a noun. In the empty boxes at the bottom, write three nouns of your own choice from the story.

Is it a noun?	Yes/No (tick if yes)	Is it a noun?	Yes/No (tick if yes)	Is it a noun?	Yes/No (tick if yes)
way		interesting		nervous	
was		dream		office	
bed		their		things	

2 Find **six** nouns in each of these extracts from the story. Draw a circle around each word that you think is a noun.

a. One day Tom decided it was time for a change. He had come up with a way to make life more interesting.

b. When Tom woke up, he decided that his bed was not a bed but a spaceship. That caused a bit of confusion.

c. She gave Tom a look even more loaded with disapproval than her earlier glare. He didn't notice – he was too busy thinking of new names for the windows.

B. Proper nouns

A **proper noun** is a specific name for someone or something. It tells exactly which person, place or thing we are referring to. For example, a proper noun may be a personal name, a place name, a day of the week or a month of the year. It always begins with a capital letter.

---

1 In each of these sentences, at least one of the nouns is a proper noun and needs a capital letter. Put a capital letter in each place that it is needed.

a. The family cat, sunny, was renamed rainy.

b. Then dad's toyota car became a realota.

c. Next, tom's school became seahear instead of hillview.

d. His class teacher was called mrs jackson.

e. But tom said, 'Good morning mrs jilldaughter.'

f. The headmaster, mr sharp, walked into the classroom.

2 Put each proper noun from the list in a gap in one of the sentences below to make it fit with the people and places in the story. Use a capital letter at the start of each proper noun.

Mum	Rainy	Toyota
Hillview	Sunny	Blunt

a. Tom called the headmaster Mr _____ .

b. Tom's school was called _____ .

c. _____ said, 'Have you made your bed, Tom?'

d. The car that Dad drove was a _____ .

e. The family cat, _____ , was really bad tempered.

f. _____ was a better name for the cat.

C. Common nouns

A **common noun** is a general name for a person, place or thing; it is less specific than a proper noun. It does not need a capital letter unless it appears at the start of a sentence.

---

1 Match each specific proper noun on the left to the more general common noun that also fits the person, place or thing that is identified. Draw a line to link each pair.

Proper noun	Common noun
Hillview	teacher
Sunny	boy
Mrs Jackson	school
Mum	father
Tom	headmaster
Mr Blunt	car
Dad	cat
Toyota	mother

2 Circle as many common nouns as you can in this extract from the story. You should circle **at least six** words but you may be able to find as many as nine common nouns.

There was a nervous giggle from one of the girls in the class but otherwise everything went very quiet. The silence was broken by Mr Sharp giving a small cough, and then saying, 'Mrs Jackson, I think Tom should come along to my office for a little chat about sensible behaviour.'

D. Place the nouns

Nouns name things. The right noun must be in the right place in a sentence. Otherwise the sentence will not make sense.

The list below includes some proper nouns (without their capital letters) and some common nouns. In the following passage, find a place that makes sense for each of these nouns and that fits with what happens in the story. If it is a proper noun, give it a capital letter.

twist	tom	things	sunny	cat
hillview	names	school	bed	rainy
dream	name	opposite	mum	sea

1 _____ had fun making up new 2 _____

for everything. He started by calling his 3 _____ a

spaceship. That was because he had just had a 4 _____

about being in a spaceship. That confused Tom's 5 _____ .

After that, he started giving 6 _____ new names that

had a 7 _____ . They were all the 8 _____

of the real names. That meant that the 9 _____

called 10 _____ became 11 _____ and

Tom's 12 _____ was Seahear instead of

13 _____ . In a way, that

14 _____ was okay because

you could hear the 15 _____

from the school as well as see the hills.

2. THE THING IS …

The thing was, Marsha wanted to get fit. She was going to play hockey and she wanted to be fit before the season started. But the other thing was, she wasn't sure about the best way to train. It took Marsha a few tries to decide what methods were not for her. But in the end she found out what **was** for her.

First Marsha tried going for a run. She put on running shoes and ran down the road, once around the park and back to her house again. Then she sat on the steps and had a think.

'The thing is,' said Marsha, 'running has never been my favourite sport. It makes me puff and I feel like a fool. Maybe I should try walking.'

So the next day, Marsha went for a walk. She put on walking shoes and walked down the road, once around the park and back to her house again. Then she sat on the steps and had another think.

'The thing is,' said Marsha, 'walking is okay if I'm going some place special. But when I'm just walking for the sake of a walk, boredom sets in. Maybe riding a bike would be more interesting.'

So the day after that, Marsha went for a bike ride. She borrowed her brother's bike, put on a cycle helmet and rode down the road, once around the park and back to her house again.

Later, as she sat on the steps having a think, Marsha said, 'The thing is, biking is quite cool, but I don't know how to mend a puncture or fix a broken chain or adjust the gears. If anything goes wrong with my bike, I can't ride it. I need something with less complicated technology to get me fit.'

Just then, the phone rang. It was her friend, Cissy, asking Marsha if she wanted to go for a swim.

'Why not?' said Marsha.

She found her swimming costume and away she went to the local pool with Cissy. When she got back from her swim, Marsha sat down on the step.

'The thing is,' Marsha said, 'swimming is wonderful! It doesn't make me puff, it isn't boring and I don't need any technology to do it. What a relief! I've found my favourite way to get fit.'

And the thing was … she had! Nearly every day after that, Marsha went swimming. She had a lot of fun and she improved her fitness too. And the curious thing is … that's the finish of this story.

Work on your ... concrete nouns and abstract nouns

As well as being proper or common, a noun may be:

- a **concrete** noun, which is a name for something you can see or touch, or

- an **abstract** noun, which is a name for something you can't directly see or touch such as an emotion.

A. What's the difference?

Concrete, meaning the material we use to build things, is a good example of a concrete noun. You can use your senses to find out more about it. For example, you can see it, touch it, feel it. It probably even has a smell and a taste although maybe it doesn't have its own sound. So a **concrete noun** names something that you can put your hand on and say 'This is the concrete' (or whatever the thing is).

An abstract noun names something that you can't directly see and touch. For example, emotions, attitudes and ideas are abstract. You may be able to see and hear someone's *happiness* because they are smiling and laughing but you can't hold *happiness* in your hand. Or someone may be talking clearly and fluently, showing great *confidence*, but you can't look at or touch a thing called *confidence*.

Here are some nouns – you can say *the* in front of each one of these words and it will make sense; it names something. For each of these nouns, decide whether it is concrete or abstract. If you think it is **concrete**, draw a line to link it with the hand. If you think it is **abstract**, draw a line to link it with the thought bubble. There are five of each type of noun.

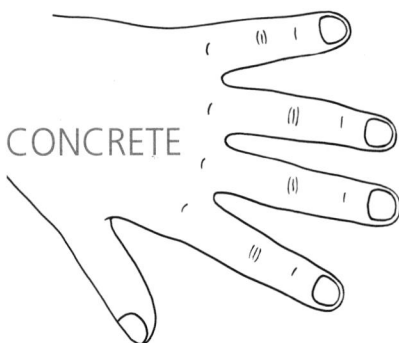

CONCRETE

ABSTRACT

day	road	method	park	house
boredom	shoes	thought	steps	way

B. Set in concrete

Concrete nouns are names for things all around us – things that we can see and touch, and maybe hear, taste and smell as well.

Concrete nouns are some of the first words we learn to say. They are the names of things around us. A concrete noun is often the answer to the question, *What's that?* We sometimes ask a small child this question when they are learning to talk. The child may say *dog* or *car* or *cup* – all things that we can see and touch and give a name. Their names are concrete nouns.

Draw a line from each concrete noun listed below to the thing that it names in the picture.

> **Hint**: Only **some** of the nouns in the list are concrete nouns.

helmet   fun   hand   speech   chain

phone   season   bike   hair   cat

C. Extract the abstract

Abstract nouns name things that you cannot directly see or touch, though you may be able to sense when they are present. For instance, you may be able to see and hear *sleep* because of the behaviour of the person who is having it, but you cannot hold the thing called *sleep* in your hands.

---

1 Below are some abstract nouns that all start with *f* – just for fun. Write each noun in the sentence in which it fits best.

fitness	friendship	favourite	fool	fun

a. Marsha and Cissy had a great _____ .

b. Marsha felt like a _____ when she ran.

c. As a get-fit activity, swimming was her _____ .

d. Marsha's _____ needed some work.

e. She found swimming was lots of _____ .

2 Many feelings are abstract nouns. In many cases we can make a word into an abstract noun to name an emotion. For example, *happy* can become *happiness*. Fill in the right-hand column in the table below by making each word on the left into an abstract noun. The first one has been done for you.

> **Hint:** To check that what you are writing is a noun, try putting the word in this sentence. If it makes sense, the word is probably a noun:
>
> I was full of _____ when I heard the news.

Original word	Abstract noun	Original word	Abstract noun
sad	*sadness*		
a. bored		d. interesting	
b. excited		e. curious	
c. wonderful		f. relieved	

D. Will it be A or C?

You use concrete nouns and abstract nouns all the time. They help you give a name to many things in your life, including people, objects, feelings and ideas. Often, of course, you don't think about whether what you are naming is concrete or abstract. But once you know the difference you can work it out.

---

1) For each noun in the list below, write C above it if it is concrete and write A above it if it is abstract.

shoes	phone	bike	day	favourite
fun	relief	pool	steps	fitness

2) Place each noun from the list above in the right place in the passage below so that it all makes sense.

When the a _____ rang, it was Cissy, asking

Marsha if she wanted to go for a swim at the local

b _____. When she got back, Marsha sat down

on the c _____ . 'The thing is,' Marsha said,

'swimming is my d _____! I don't have to put on

my running e _____ and I don't have to ride a

f _____ . What a g _____!

I've found a way to get fit.' And the thing

was … she had! Nearly every

h _____ after that,

Marsha went swimming. She had a lot

of i _____ and she

improved her j _____

too.

3. IT'S A HE

'It's not an *it*, it's a *he*,' said Laurie.

'I don't care if it's it, she, he or whatever. Take that stray cat out of the house right now!'

Mum's reaction may have seemed a bit harsh, but Laurie knew that it was probably fair enough. She was always bringing home stray animals of all sorts. If Mum had let her keep every one of them inside, their house would be now more like a zoo or an animal refuge than a home for people. Laurie tucked the scrawny cat under one arm, picked up the dish of milk and walked outside.

She put the cat and the dish down on the veranda and watched as the cat went back to greedily licking up the milk. It (really *he*, Laurie thought to herself) seemed to be really hungry. Laurie considered what to do. She'd found the cat scavenging around rubbish bins at the back of the local shops. It was quite friendly, and meowed and came running when Laurie called to it. Maybe it wasn't really a stray but someone's pet that had got lost.

When the cat had licked the bowl clean, Laurie picked it up and decided she would knock on a few doors in the neighbourhood and see if anyone had lost a cat. She popped her head in through the back door first and told Mum where she was going. The cat, now that it was full of milk, was quite happy to be snuggled in Laurie's arms. It was purring and half closing its eyes. It seemed so tame. Laurie spent the next hour knocking on doors in her neighbourhood but no one was missing a cat. She was just about to go home when she saw someone coming toward her.

It was an elderly man, walking slowly and stopping to look into every yard he passed. He was so busy doing this that he did not see Laurie until he was right in front of her. Even then, it was not Laurie he noticed but the cat snuggled in her arms.

'Tiger!' said the old man. 'Where have you been?'

The cat immediately woke up when it heard the man's voice. It jumped happily into the man's arms, smooching against his face and purring loudly. The elderly man turned to Laurie.

'Thank you so much for finding our Tiger,' he said. 'I really thought we'd lost him for good.'

Laurie could see that Tiger had a good home to go to – a home where he was loved and looked after. She was happy to see that. What's more, she knew Mum would be **very** happy that the cat's home wasn't hers!

Work on your ... pronouns

A **pronoun** can take the place of a noun. It saves you from repeating the same noun too many times close together.

When you are reading a sentence that uses a pronoun, you need to know which noun the pronoun is replacing in order to get the full meaning from the sentence.

A. This noun, that pronoun

The most common pronouns we use are **personal pronouns**. A personal pronoun refers back to someone or something that has already been mentioned. We must know exactly who or what the pronoun refers back to; otherwise, we can get confused.

In the story, the pronouns *she, he* and *it* are all used:

- *She* could be Laurie or her mother.

- *He* is the elderly man. The cat might also be *he* – Laurie thinks the cat is *he* although we usually refer to an animal as *it*.

- *It* is the cat when Laurie is not the person using the personal pronoun for it. *It* can also replace other nouns that are things rather than people – such as the dish or the milk in the story.

In each sentence on the left, circle the pronoun. Next, draw a line to match each sentence with the noun on the right that can replace its pronoun.

Pronoun sentence	Matching noun
1. The cat went back to greedily licking it up.	Laurie
2. It was quite happy to be snuggled in Laurie's arms.	Mum
3. He was walking slowly and stopping to look into every yard.	the cat
4. She was always bringing home stray animals of all sorts.	the man
5. Laurie put it down on the veranda and watched as the cat licked up the milk provided.	the dish
6. She wanted the stray cat out of the house now.	the milk

B. Busy pronouns

A **subject pronoun** is a pronoun that replaces a noun that is the subject of a sentence. The **subject** is the person or thing doing the action in a sentence.

The chart below shows the personal pronouns that you use as the subject of a sentence. You will see from this chart that we can categorise these pronouns based on how many people or things are involved as the subject:

- **singular** – when the subject is one person or thing
- **plural** – when the subject is two or more people or things.

We can also categorise the pronouns based on subject's point of view:

- **first person** – when the subject is the person who writing or speaking
- **second person** – when the subject is the person who is being written or spoken to
- **third person** – when the subject is anyone else other than the speaker, writer or the person being addressed.

Subject pronouns

	Singular	Plural
1st person	I	we
2nd person	you	you
3rd person	he / she / it	they

Note: For more information about action in sentences, see 'Work on your … verbs' (chapter 5) and the next book in this series, *Book 2: Building sentences*.

These sentences need fixing. Can you do it? Cross out the wrong pronoun in each sentence and write the correct one above it.

1. Laurie said, 'Okay, he will take the cat outside.'

2. The neighbours all said it had not lost a cat.

3. 'They do not need that cat in our house,' said Mum.

4. Mum said, 'She did well, Laurie, to find the cat's owner.'

5. The man was delighted when they saw the cat.

6. Laurie knew you brought too many stray animals home.

C. It happened to …

An **object pronoun** replaces a noun that is the object of a sentence. The **object** is the person or thing affected by the action in a sentence.

The chart below shows the personal pronouns that you use for the object of a sentence. Like subject pronouns, personal pronouns can be singular or plural, and first, second or third person.

Object pronouns

	Singular	**Plural**
1st person	me	us
2nd person	you	you
3rd person	him / her / it	them

In the caption for each picture below, a pronoun is missing. Fill each gap with a suitable pronoun from the chart of object pronouns above.

1. The dish had milk in _____ .

3. 'I want to thank _____ ,' said the man.

2. 'The cat likes _____ ,' said Laurie.

4. Laurie gave the cat to _____ .

21

D. Pronouns that say who owns

A **possessive pronoun** tells you who owns something. To make your message clear, you have to use the right possessive pronoun.

The chart below shows some pronouns and the possessive pronoun that goes with each one.

Pronouns and their matching possessive pronouns

Pronoun	I	you	he	she	it	we	they
Possessive pronoun	my	your	his	her	its	our	their

---

1 From the chart above, find a possessive pronoun that fits in the gap in each of the following sentences. Check that the pronoun you choose makes sense in that sentence, and in terms of what happens in the story.

a. The man knew straight away that it was _____ cat.

b. The neighbours had not lost _____ cat.

c. 'I took the cat to _____ home first,' said Laurie.

d. 'I really appreciate _____ help,' said the man.

e. Laurie told _____ mother where she was going.

f. The cat opened _____ eyes when it heard the man.

g. 'It's nice to have _____ house to ourselves,' said Mum.

2 In this paragraph, three possessive pronouns are wrong. Cross out each one that is wrong and write the correct pronoun above it.

The cat jumped happily into the

man's arms, smooching against

her face and purring loudly. The elderly man turned to Laurie. 'I

thank your lucky stars that you found their Tiger,' he said.

4. THIS MAGIC PLACE

Hi Chris

We got to this magic place last night, in the dark. It's a beautiful sunny day this morning so I've had a good look around the spot where we'll spend the next four days. I have to write to you and tell you what it is like. You would totally love it here!

The old house where we are staying sits on the edge of a lush green forest. It's a little way above the road, so you get a great view out to sea as well. The beach is across the other side of the bumpy shingle road. It's a rugged windswept beach, a jumble of rocks and stones and sand with huge breakers rolling in. Last night you could hear the boulders rolling in the surf with an amazingly deep, grinding sound.

This morning the swell has died down a bit and, with the sun shining on the water, it's all blue and glittering. We even saw a small group of about six dolphins playing out there first thing   – that seemed like such a special gift. I have already been for a walk down the beach this morning, where I found plenty of awesome rocks and shells and bits of gnarly driftwood. I'll try to sort out some good bits to bring back for you.

Later today we're going for a walk or maybe a mountain bike ride. There's a narrow, winding forest track that follows the rocky river inland, starting right out here near the wide mouth of the river. Matt has ridden it before and he says it's fantastic. It goes up through the forest, crossing a few smaller streams along the way, and gradually climbing up into the hills. I think it goes right up to an old hut, some historic place that's supposed to be a bit worse for wear, but we might not get that far – we'll try to get most of the way at least.

There's probably good fishing here, in the river or surfcasting off the beach. I'm not that keen on fishing but I know you are and you'd probably be out there with your fishing rod right now. Hopefully the little cafe down the road will have fresh local fish on the menu – I might not like catching fish but I do like eating it! Anyway I hear they do fantastic coffee and more varieties of fruit smoothies than anyone else in the country so we'll be paying the cafe at least one visit.

This break would be even better if you were here to share it all with us. I'll take plenty of photos to show you and hopefully you will get to see it all for yourself before too long.

See you soon.
Roz xxx

Work on your ... adjectives

An **adjective** is a word that describes a noun or a pronoun. It adds more information about a person, place or thing. It usually comes immediately before the noun or pronoun it describes but sometimes it appears later in the sentence.

A. Spot the adjectives

In these extracts from the story, draw a circle around each adjective. There are five adjectives in each extract.

> **Hint:** Finding the nouns first will help you find the adjectives. (Check back to chapters 1 and 2 if you want to revise nouns.)

1. We got to this magic place last night, in the dark. I woke up to a beautiful sunny day this morning so I could have a good look around.

2. The old house where we are staying sits on the edge of a lush green forest. It's a little way above the road, so you get a great view out to sea as well.

3. There's a narrow, winding track that follows the rocky river inland, starting right out here near the wide mouth of the river. Matt has ridden it before and he says it's fantastic.

B. Some adjectives

Adjectives give different details about nouns. Some tell us about the number, amount or size of a noun – that is, they are concerned with **quantity or measurement**.

Numbers are the most obvious adjectives that describe quantity. For example, you will find *four days, six dolphins, one visit* in the story.

Here are some adjectives that provide information about quantity. Fit each one in one of the gaps in the captions for the pictures below.

gnarly	huge	small	plenty	wide	narrow

1. A _____ group of dolphins

4. The _____ river mouth

2. The _____ breakers

5. Bits of _____ driftwood

3. _____ of awesome rocks

6. A _____ forest track

C. Which one?

Some adjectives help us to ask for or give information:

- An adjective can ask us something, such as *which*? or *what*? It is asking us to fill in more details about a noun. This kind of adjective is an **interrogative adjective**. Interrogative means questioning. (For more information about questions, see *Book 2: Building sentences* in this series.)

- An adjective can provide an answer by pointing something out, such as *this* or *that*. This kind of adjective is a **demonstrative adjective**. It demonstrates an answer by pointing it out.

Each question on the left uses an interrogative adjective to ask something about the story. Draw a line to link each of these questions to the answer on the right that fits with what happens in the story. Each answer uses a demonstrative adjective.

Question	Answer
1. Which house is Roz staying in?	a. Those boulders rolling in the surf.
2. What is making the deep, grinding sound?	b. That narrow track by the river.
3. Which café does fantastic coffee?	c. This magic place.
4. What is Roz bringing back for Chris?	d. That old house on the edge of the forest.
5. Which track has Matt ridden before?	e. These rocks and shells and bits of driftwood.
6. What does Roz call the place she is visiting?	f. This little café down the road.

D. More of that, please

Sometimes an adjective can help us to tell things apart. It can tell us when a certain characteristic is more intense or stronger in one example than in another – eg, yesterday was a *sunny* day, today is a *sunnier* day, tomorrow will be the *sunniest* day of all. Notice that in all these examples, the noun is the same. It is the change to the adjective that shows the difference between two things of the same kind, even when they are very similar.

So we can use an adjective to compare things. It can be:

- a **comparative adjective**, which compares two things – we usually make it by adding *-er* to the ordinary adjective or else by adding *more* if *-er* doesn't sound right (see the middle column of the chart below)

- a **superlative adjective**, which points out the thing that has more of one quality than any other – we usually make it by adding *-est* to the ordinary adjective or else by adding *most* if *-est* doesn't sound right (see the right-hand column of the chart below).

The chart below gives some examples of ordinary, comparative and superlative adjectives. Fill in each gap with the correct form of the adjective. The first ones have been done for you.

> **Hint:** For answers in the middle and right-hand columns, you will add *-er, -est, more* or *most*. For answers in the left-hand column, you will take off one of these signs of a comparative or superlative form.

Some examples of ordinary, comparative and superlative adjectives

Ordinary adjective	Comparative adjective	Superlative adjective
beautiful	*more beautiful*	*most beautiful*
old	*older*	oldest
	greater	
winding		
		deepest
special		
awesome		
	gnarlier	
		most fantastic
	bumpier	

E. Extra special adjectives

Some adjectives don't use -er or -est, more or most. Instead they have completely different words for their comparative and superlative forms. The chart below gives some examples of these special adjectives.

Examples of special adjectives: ordinary, comparative and superlative forms

Ordinary adjective	Comparative adjective	Superlative adjective
good	better	best
bad	worse	worst
many / much	more	most
little / few	less	least

For each of these sentences, fill in the gap with one of the comparative or superlative adjectives in the chart above. Make your choices consistent with what happens in the story. You may use each form of each adjective only once.

1. People say the old hut is a bit _____ for wear.

2. We'll try to bike most of the way there at _____.

3. The _____ thing about staying at the hut is that it doesn't have a shower.

4. The local café has the _____ smoothies I have ever tasted.

5. The quality is _____ than I expected from a little café in the middle of nowhere.

6. It also has the _____ beautiful view that I have ever seen.

7. Our holiday would be even _____ if you were here.

8. Maybe next time you will have _____ work to do so you could come with us.

5. ACTION STATIONS

Alfie Acton likes to be active. He is always thinking of new things to do. Each day of the week he has a different way of getting to work. On Mondays Alfie rides his skateboard to work. He finds that's a good way to start the week so Mondays don't seem so boring. On his skateboard he can whiz down the hill from his house then use the cycle lane section of the footpath around the waterfront to roll into town.

On Tuesdays Alfie cycles to work. That is mainly because he has football practice after work on a Tuesday and he can get there much more quickly on his bike. He can slip through the city traffic when cars and buses are often stuck in a rush-hour traffic jam. He can also use cycle lanes and take the odd shortcut through parks. Alfie likes to be on the move. He pedals hard and fast when he is biking.

On Wednesdays Alfie usually walks to work. He finds that is a good way to stretch out his leg muscles after football training the night before. He can go a different way too, following some steps up and over the hill into town instead of down to the main road and around. It doesn't take too much longer and it's quieter.

On Thursdays Alfie likes to do something quite different. He has a kayak stored in a friend's shed down near the water. He pulls that out and uses it to paddle along by the seafront to the town centre. He really enjoys using his arm muscles for a change and it's great looking over to his left and seeing all the traffic struggling along the road.

On Fridays Alfie takes the bus to work. Sometimes he finds this a bit hard as it means sitting still for longer than he likes. But he figures it is a way of reminding himself how much more fun he has on the other days. Also, he is storing up some extra energy for all the activities he has planned for the weekend.

This Saturday Alfie plans to go kite surfing in the morning and BMX riding in the afternoon. On Sunday he is going to compete in a triathlon. He's an active kind of guy, that Alfie Acton. Oh, and by the way, if you were wondering what kind of work he goes to do each day – he's an abseiling window cleaner for all the high-rise buildings in town. He's always on the go.

Work on your ... verbs

A **verb** can be one word or sometimes a group of words. A sentence does not make sense without a verb. The verb tells us what is happening in a sentence, what someone or something is doing or being (or has done or will do ... etc). Verbs catch the action.

A. Spot the action

1. Circle the verbs in each of the following sentences from the story. Remember, you are looking for the action.

a. On Tuesdays Alfie cycles to work.

t.

b. He has football practice after work on a Tuesday.

u.

c. He can get there much more quickly on his bike.

v.

d. He can slip through the city traffic.

e. Cars and buses are stuck in a rush-hour traffic jam.

w.

f. Alfie can use cycle lanes.

x.

g. He takes the odd shortcut through parks.

y.

h. Alfie likes to be on the move.

i. He pedals hard and fast.

z.

2. Look at what is happening in the pictures on the right. Draw a line from each picture to link with the sentence in Question 1 that best describes the action.

B. The name of the action

Verbs have a base name, called the **infinitive** form of the verb. The infinitive usually has the word *to* in front of it – eg, *to be, to start, to paddle, to go, to compete*. From this base name, we form other verbs, which can look quite different from the infinitive. For example, some of the verb forms that we can make from the infinitive *to go* are *goes, will go* and *went*.

For each infinitive verb on the right, draw two lines to link it to two sentences where that action is being used.

Infinitive verb	Example sentence
	a. More people are cycling these days.
1. To have	b. Alfie was walking to work last Wednesday.
	c. Alfie and his friends plan to go kite surfing.
2. To cycle	d. Alfie has a kayak in a friend's shed.
3. To stretch	e. Alfie will walk to work next Wednesday.
	f. Not many people enjoy traffic jams.
4. To enjoy	g. His muscles are stretching.
	h. He will have a bus ride on Friday.
5. To plan	i. Alfie cycles to work on Tuesdays.
	j. Alfie will stretch after football.
	k. Alfie enjoyed his BMX ride.
6. To walk	l. He is planning to give up his abseiling job.

C. Who did that?

The form of a verb has to match the subject. The **subject** is the person or thing doing the action in a sentence. The **form of verb** we use depends on whether the subject is:

- singular or plural

- first, second or third person.(For more information about singular and plural, and about first, second and third person, look at 'Work on your … pronouns' in chapter 3.)

The first chart below shows how one verb changes from its infinitive form – *to like*. In general, the form of this verb looks the same as the infinitive. The only different form is for the third person singular, which has an *s* on the end. This pattern is common for verbs. (We are focusing on the present tense for now.)

Changes in form for the verb: to like

Person	Singular	Plural
1st	I like	We like
2nd	You like	You like
3rd	She / he / it likes	They like

However, some verbs change their form a lot. Look at what the verb *to be* does in the next chart.

Changes in form for the verb: to be

Person	Singular	Plural
1st	I am	We are
2nd	You are	You are
3rd	She / he / is	They are

Put the right verb in each of these sentences. Choose verbs from the charts above.

1. Alfie wonders how many people _____ traffic jams.

2. This morning, Alfie _____ biking to work.

3. 'I _____ action,' says Alfie.

4. 'I _____ kayaking to work today,' says Alfie.

5. 'You _____ crazy if you always drive to work,' says Alfie.

6. Alfie _____ being an abseiling window cleaner.

D. Time to do things

The verb can tell you when something is happening. This time zone is known as the **tense** of the verb. There are many tenses. The three main ones are:

- the **present** (now)
- the **past** (before now) – which for many verbs we make by adding -*ed* to the end
- the **future** (it will happen but it hasn't yet) – which we make by adding *will* in front of the main verb.

Each verb in the chart below has been written in all three of these tenses. Can you see how some verbs follow the pattern for past tense and future tense noted above? Can you see two verbs that are **not** part of this pattern?

Present	Past	Future
Alfie works.	Alfie worked.	Alfie will work.
Alfie pedals.	Alfie pedalled.	Alfie will pedal.
Alfie goes.	Alfie went.	Alfie will go.
Alfie looks.	Alfie looked.	Alfie will look.
Alfie thinks.	Alfie thought.	Alfie will think.

Place the right verb from the chart in each gap below.

> **Hint:** Read each sentence carefully to see if it is happening in the present, the past or the future. That will help you choose the right verb.

1. Alfie _____ to work on his bike on Tuesdays now.

2. Alfie _____ at the traffic jam as he paddled past.

3. Alfie _____ to a BMX event last summer.

4. Alfie _____ as a window cleaner at present.

5. Alfie _____ taking the bus to work was not good.

6. Alfie _____ of a new way to go to work next week.

6. YOU DID THAT?

'Do you honestly have to play that music so loudly?' said Gran as she stood in the doorway.

Kit very reluctantly turned the stereo down. It didn't seem totally fair. Kit was playing the stereo in his own room, and Mum and Dad didn't usually mind if it was that loud. But since Gran had arrived, things had changed dramatically.

It wasn't that Kit really minded having Gran around. She had been living alone but lately she'd had a few health problems so Mum and Dad had asked her to come and stay, just until she was feeling better. That was fine – there was plenty of room in their house and it was good to help Gran out. But Kit hadn't actually realised how much he'd have to change with Gran living in the house.

Having to turn the stereo down was only the start. At dinnertime, Kit now had to sit at the table to eat with Mum, Dad and Gran. He couldn't eat in front of the telly any more, or read a magazine or a book while he was eating. Gran didn't even like the radio on. She said it interfered with conversation. Mum and Dad were happy to go along with that. In fact, Dad said, 'This is how we should have meals all the time. It's a good chance for some real family time. So, how was your day, Kit?'

At first Kit found it a bit odd, chatting about his day and how he had to plan a big project for school, while they were eating dinner. But after a couple of days he began getting used to the new mealtime pattern. One of the best things was that Gran started talking about when she was his age. When she had first said, 'Now when I was at school …' Kit thought it would be mega boring but he soon found himself eagerly listening to everything Gran said. Dinnertime went by so quickly, they ended up sitting around the table, talking and laughing easily for another hour at least. Kit even missed one of his favourite TV programmes and he didn't mind at all.

Later that evening, Kit suddenly thought of a good idea. He went into the lounge where Gran was sitting on the couch, quietly looking through some old photo albums.

'Gran, can I ask you something?' said Kit politely.

And that was when he sorted out what he was going to do for his major class project – he was going to record an oral history interview with Gran, about what school was like in her day. Kit fully realised he was really happy that Gran had come to stay.

Work on your ... adverbs

The term **adverb** tells you that an adverb can add information to a verb. You have seen that a verb tells us what happens; an adverb tells us much more about **how** it happens.

A. Verb plus adverb

An adverb can tell us **how, when, where** or even **why** something is happening. Two clues that can help you to spot one are:

- finding the verb in a sentence (ie, by finding the action) as the verb should point you to the adverb
- knowing that many adverbs end with *-ly* (eg, *madly, finally*). Note, though, that some words that end in *-ly* are **not** adverbs (eg, *holly, silly*).

---

1 In each of the following sentences, circle the adverb or adverbs. One sentence has two adverbs. One has no adverb at all.

> **Hint:** Some of the *-ly* words are adverbs but some are not. Check that an *-ly* word is adding information to a verb before you circle it.

a. 'Do you honestly have to play that music so loudly?'

b. Mum and Dad didn't usually mind.

c. Kit hadn't actually realised how much he'd have to change.

d. Having to turn the stereo down was only the start.

e. He couldn't eat in front of the telly any more.

f. Kit suddenly thought of a good idea.

2 Here is a list of adverbs that don't end in *-ly*. Choose three of the six sentences above and replace the adverbs with new ones from the list. Your new sentences may change the meaning but they must still make sense.

never	just	soon	ever	still	often

a.———————————————————————————

b.———————————————————————————

c.———————————————————————————

B. What else can an adverb add?

Adverbs are useful as **describing words**. Although they usually add information to verbs, they can also add to other adverbs, adjectives, prepositions and conjunctions. Here are some examples of how we can use an adverb to add information to words other than verbs:

Kit very reluctantly turned the stereo down.
very (adverb) adds to *reluctantly* (adverb)

It didn't seem totally fair.
totally (adverb) adds to *fair* (adjective)

We can make many adverbs from an adjective, usually by adding -*ly* to the adjective. This can mean changing the spelling at the end of the adjective. The chart gives some examples.

Making an adverb from an adjective: some examples

Adjective	Adverb
usual	usually
reluctant	reluctantly
dramatic	dramatically
eager	eagerly
easy	easily
full	fully

1. In the chart above, which three adverbs have been created by changing the spelling in a more substantial way than simply adding -*ly*? How has the spelling changed for each one?

_____

_____

_____

2. In each of these sentences, circle the adjective that should be an adverb. Write the correct spelling on the line at the end of the sentence.

a. It wasn't that Kit real minded having Gran around. _____

b. Late she'd had a few health problems. _____

c. He found himself eager listening to all Gran said. _____

d. Dinnertime went by so quick. _____

e. They were talking and laughing for easy another hour. _____

f. Gran was quiet looking through photo albums. _____

C. Adverbs make a difference

The adverb you choose can totally change a message. Sometimes you can even change it to the opposite meaning.

Compare these sentences. Each one gives a different message.

Kit turned the stereo down.

Kit *reluctantly* turned the stereo down.

Kit *happily* turned the stereo down.

Kit *quickly* turned the stereo down.

Kit *slowly* turned the stereo down.

You can see that each adverb changes the meaning of the basic sentence a lot. In each case, the adverb makes us think about why Kit behaved like that.

In each sentence below, cross the adverb out and above it write another adverb with the opposite meaning. Choose your new adverbs from this list. You can use each one only once.

quietly	roughly	easily
rightly	slowly	fully

1. Kit partly realised he was happy that Gran had come to stay.

2. He had to carefully plan a big project for school.

3. He found he was quickly getting used to the new mealtime routine.

4. They talked tensely for an hour.

5. Gran started talking loudly about when she was his age.

6. Kit wrongly thought it would be mega boring.

D. Adverbs in their place

Where you place the adverb in a sentence can be very important. It can change the meaning of the sentence entirely.

In the left-hand column, the position of one adverb – *only* – is the **only** thing that changes in four sentences. Some of the meanings are more alike than others. Draw a line from each sentence to the meaning in the right-hand column that you think fits best.

> **Hint:** You may find it helpful to talk to someone else about the meanings of the different sentences before you make your choices.

Sentence with moving adverb	Meaning
1. Only Kit talked to Gran for an hour.	a. Kit didn't go anywhere with Gran or have a cup of tea – he just talked to her for an hour.
2. Kit talked only to Gran for an hour.	b. Kit talked to Gran for one hour, no longer than that, and that probably wasn't enough.
3. Kit talked to Gran for only an hour.	c. Nobody else except Kit spoke to Gran for an hour.
4. Kit only talked to Gran for an hour.	d. For a whole hour, Kit talked to nobody but Gran.

Extra adverb challenge

Add the adverb *suddenly* to this sentence. Try moving it around so that you create as many different meanings as possible.

Kit realised he was happy that Gran had come to stay.

_____

_____

_____

_____

_____

7. IN A PANIC

Across the other side of the room, Bea could see the thing she wanted above everything else. However, between her and this thing that she really, really wanted was a whole crowd of people and any one of those people might get to the thing before she could. Bea launched herself into the throng. She was on a quest.

Bea hadn't realised that the jumble sale would be quite this busy. The community hall was packed. It was raining outside and that made a difference too. Some stalls that would have been set up outside had moved indoors as well, so it was all crammed in together. Bea had climbed onto a chair to get a good look around. Now she was anxiously pushing her way through the crowd to get to the other side of the room.

What Bea was aiming for was a second-hand clothing stall. The thing she wanted was hanging on the wall behind the stall so she was catching glimpses of it as she made her way across the room. She was almost there. One more group of people to get past and she would able to reach out and hold it. But … oh no! She couldn't believe it: she was standing in front of the stall but the thing she wanted so much had gone from the wall. Bea was frantic. Where had it gone in such a short time?

The woman serving at the stall smiled at Bea. Bea found it hard to speak. She pointed at the wall space where the thing had been hanging and said, 'Where did it go?' The woman looked behind her at the wall. She knew immediately what Bea was talking about and pointed toward someone who was disappearing into the crowd just a short distance away. Bea gasped. Maybe there was hope after all.

'Mum!' she called as she rushed after the disappearing figure. Bea's mother turned around and Bea could see that in her hand was that precious thing. 'You got it back!' said Bea as she caught up with her mother.

'Yes,' said Mum. 'I didn't realise till this morning just how attached you were to it and I felt bad about giving it away for the jumble sale. So here you are.'

She passed the thing over to Bea who grabbed it eagerly and hugged it tight. She wasn't going to lose her absolutely favourite T-shirt again in a hurry, especially not to a jumble sale!

Work on your ... prepositions and conjunctions

Prepositions and conjunctions are useful 'building-block' words. They can link ideas or words in a sentence. Both of these parts of speech help to make your writing flow well.

A. Recognition of prepositions

To identify a **preposition**, we cannot just look for a particular word such as *in, on, over* or *under*. Many prepositions are also adverbs or conjunctions. So how can we tell when a word is a preposition? We have to look at what it is doing in the sentence. Here are some clues to look for:

- Prepositions **always** come before nouns or pronouns.

- Prepositions show the **position** of something in space or time.

The following extract from the story includes three prepositions in **bold**. Each one comes before a noun (*the wall, the stall, the room)*. All of them tell us about the position of things: where the special thing was in the hall and where Bea was walking.

> The thing she wanted was hanging **on** the wall **behind** the stall so she was catching glimpses of it as she made her way **across** the room.

Place each preposition from the list in the gap in one of the sentences below. Make the meaning agree with what happens in the story.

into	from	after	in	at	with

1. She was standing _____ the hall.

2. The thing she wanted had gone _____ the wall.

3. The woman serving _____ the stall smiled at Bea.

4. Someone was disappearing _____ the crowd.

5. She rushed _____ the disappearing figure.

6. Bea caught up _____ her mother.

B. Spot the conjunctions

We use a **conjunction** to connect ideas or words in a sentence. That is why a conjunction is sometimes called a 'joining word'. We can use it to connect two or more ideas into one longer sentence; otherwise we would have to use a number of short sentences. So conjunctions help us to avoid repeating things and to make our writing flow better.

The most common conjunction is *and*. It is a simple way of joining ideas and we use it often – sometimes we use it too much. In the next activity you can work with some other useful conjunctions.

Join each pair of sentences below with one of the conjunctions from this list. You may use each conjunction only once.

but	yet	or	so	because	while

> **Hint:** Check that the meaning of the joined sentence fits with the story.

1. Bea was at the jumble sale _____ she was looking for her T-shirt.

2. She had to get it back _____ she would be upset.

3. Bea's mum bought the shirt _____ Bea was crossing the room.

4. Mum had given the shirt to the jumble sale _____ now she was sorry about that.

5. The shirt had been there on the wall _____ now it was gone.

6. Bea really loved that shirt _____ her mum would not give it away to a jumble sale again.

Check your conjunctions

Read each pair of sentences above without the conjunction and then with the conjunction added. You will see that the ideas in the writing are much better connected with the conjunction in place.

8. PLAYING TO LEARN

Mo had enjoyed playing computer games for a while. He started playing at his friend's place but now he had a computer at home. That meant he could play much more often but his parents wouldn't let him spend more than an hour a day on games during the week. They were a bit less strict at the weekends and in the holidays. Mo sometimes wished they would just leave him to it but he knew that then he'd probably spend every free minute on the computer. That would not be healthy for his body or his brain. He did like playing when he could though.

The more Mo played, the more he began to think that he would like to invent his own game. He knew what he liked and what he didn't like about different games. He thought he knew what would work better and what sort of setting would make a game more interesting. He could play games, he had ideas about a new game, but the trouble was, he didn't know how to make one. He decided to find out more.

Mo started doing some research. He talked to one of his older cousins who was right into computer games as well.

'Oh, yeah,' said Josh. 'I used to think I'd like to write my own game too. But it all seemed too hard. You need to know about HTML – that's the language you use for typing commands into a computer. I couldn't really be bothered. I just play games.'

So Mo started finding out about this other language. He had never been keen on learning about what he called 'boring grammar' at school and yet, in a way, learning HTML was like learning a set of grammar rules. He could use computers okay, but he had never realised that understanding how computer language worked could help him so much more. The more he learnt, the more he found he could do and the more interesting he found it. He was hooked. He signed up for an after-school course on computer programming and went to it every Thursday. He even did a four-day block course during the Christmas holidays.

Soon Mo was spending about half his computer time playing games and the other half learning more about how they worked. Any day now, Mo would have his first game up and running. And already he could see how he might make the next one an even better game.

Revise your ... parts of speech

A **part of speech** means a group or category of words that does a particular job for us when we communicate. If you know what part of speech a word is in a sentence, you can tell if it is:

- a noun – it names a person, place or thing
- a pronoun – it replaces a noun
- an adjective – it describes a noun or pronoun
- a verb – it is a word for being or doing
- an adverb – it describes a verb
- a preposition – it shows where things are in relation to one another
- a conjunction – it joins words and ideas.

Here are some activities for you to practise what you have learnt about parts of speech.

A. Nouns – common and proper

Put each noun from the list in the gap in a sentence below so that it fits with what happens in the story. Use a capital letter if it is a proper noun.

mo	computer	josh	weekends	christmas	parents

1. They were a bit less strict at the _____ .

2. Now he had a _____ at home.

3. So _____ started finding out about HTML.

4. His _____ wouldn't let him spend more than an hour on games.

5. He even did a course during the _____ holidays.

6. He talked to one of his older cousins, _____ .

B. Nouns – concrete and abstract

Circle three concrete nouns and underline three abstract nouns in this passage.

> **Hint:** Each abstract noun relates to time.

At the weekends and in the holidays Mo played more often. He spent every free minute on the computer. That was not healthy for his body.

C. Pronouns

1 Circle the pronouns in this piece of writing.

Mo could play more computer games now that he had a computer at home. 'My parents won't let me spend more than an hour a day on games during the week,' said Mo. 'I suppose I should respect their opinion. What do you think? Should I ask them for more time? What do your parents say?' His friend, Gina, replied that her parents said she could only play when all homework was done but that they were a bit less strict about it at the weekends and in the holidays.

2 Place each pronoun that you circled above in the correct box of the chart. There will still be some blank boxes when you have finished. Try to fill them in using your knowledge of pronouns.

Pronouns

		Singular	Plural
1st person	Subject		
	Object		
	Possessive		
2nd person	Subject		
	Object		
	Possessive		
3rd person	Subject		
	Object		
	Possessive		

D. Adjectives

For each adjective on the left, draw a line to connect it with the noun on the right that it best describes in the story.

Adjectives	Nouns
1. older	a. game
2. two	b. grammar
3. new	c. computer
4. block	d. parents
5. boring	e. cousin
6. own	f. course

E. Verbs

For each sentence below, choose a verb from the list to complete it so that the sentence fits with the story. The list shows each verb in its infinitive form; you may have to change that form to put it in the sentence. Draw a line to link each verb to the sentence where it is used.

to enjoy	to spend	to play	to know
to have	to be	to learn	to use

1. Josh just _____ games now.

2. The course _____ on computer programming.

3. He _____ what sort of games he liked.

4. You _____ HTML to give computer commands.

5. In the past, Mo always _____ playing computer games.

6. He now _____ some ideas about a new game.

7. Mo _____ half his computer time playing and half learning.

8. Mo said, 'I _____ so much from the computer course I did last term.'

F. Adverbs

Circle the eight adverbs in this paragraph.

Mo really wanted to learn how computer games worked so he gradually built up his knowledge by doing research. Soon he was easily spending about half his computer time playing games and the other half happily learning more about how they worked technically. Any day now, Mo would successfully have his first game actually up and running. And he could already see how he might make the next one even better.

G. Prepositions

Fit each of these prepositions into a gap in the piece of writing below.

for	in	on	at	to	about

Mo had never been keen 1 _____ learning

2 _____ what he called 'boring grammar'

3 _____ school and yet, 4 _____ a way,

learning HTML was like learning a set of grammar rules. He signed

up 5 _____ an after-school course on computer

programming and went 6 _____ it every Thursday.

H. Conjunctions

Place a conjunction from this list into each gap in the following sentences. Each completed sentence should make sense and fit with what happens in the story. You may use each conjunction only once.

and	yet	so	after	because
until	then	but	when	before

1. Mo wanted to write a game _____ he learnt HTML.

2. He talked to Josh _____ he started the course.

3. He was allowed to play games _____ not all day.

4. Mo knew what he liked _____ what he didn't like.

5. Mo played games _____ he enjoyed them.

6. He found the rules more interesting _____ he could see how they helped him.

7. Mo learnt things _____ he used them to make his game better.

8. He was having fun _____ he was learning too.

9. Mo was always full of ideas _____ he came home from the class.

10. Mo would keep playing and writing games _____ he was tired of them.

I. Make it all better

The piece of writing below has quite a few mistakes. Many parts of speech need fixing.

Write it out again in the space below and fix all the mistakes. You will see that, when you use parts of speech correctly, you can make it all make sense!

> **Hint:** Sometimes the meaning here is completely opposite to what it should be. Check the story if you are unsure of what any part of this paragraph should mean.

Mo begun to thought that she would liked to inventor my own games. They knewed what you likes and that him didn't like of same gaming. He to think he knows what would work worse but whatever sorting of set wouldn't make a games morer interestinger.

ACTIVITY ANSWERS

1. Work on your … proper and common nouns

A1. way, bed, dream, office, things *(Ask someone else to check the three other nouns you have chosen.)*

A2. a. day, Tom, time, change, way, life
b. Tom, bed, bed, spaceship, bit, confusion
c. Tom, look, disapproval, glare, names, windows

B1. a. Sunny, Rainy
b. Dad's, Toyota, Realota
c. Tom's, Seahear, Hillview
d. Mrs Jackson
e. Tom, Mrs Jilldaughter
f. Mr Sharp

B2. a. Blunt
b. Hillview
c. Mum
d. Toyota
e. Sunny
f. Rainy

C1. Hillview – school
Sunny – cat
Mrs Jackson – teacher
Mum – mother
Tom – boy
Dad – father
Mr Blunt – headmaster
Toyota – car

C2. *At least six words from:*
giggle, girls, class, everything, silence, cough, office, chat, behaviour

(continued)

1. Work on your … proper and common nouns (continued)

D. 1. Tom
2. names
3. bed
4. dream
5. mum *(only a proper noun when it acts like someone's name – eg, 'Hey Mum!')*
6. things
7. twist
8. opposite
9. cat
10. Sunny
11. Rainy
12. school
13. Hillview
14. name
15. sea

(Note: Make sure the proper nouns have capital letters.)

2. Work on your … concrete and abstract nouns

A. *Concrete (hand):* road, park, house, shoes, steps

Abstract (thought bubble): day, method, boredom, thought, way

B. *Draw links for:* helmet, hand, chain, phone, bike, hair, cat

C1. a. friendship
b. fool
c. favourite
d. fitness
e. fun

C2. a. boredom
b. excitement
c. wonder
d. interest
e. curiosity
f. relief

D1. *Concrete (C):* shoes, phone, bike, pool, steps

Abstract (A): day, favourite, fun, relief, fitness

D2. a. phone
b. pool
c. steps
d. favourite
e. shoes
f. bike
g. relief
h. day
i. fun
j. fitness

3. Work on your … pronouns

A. 1. it – the milk
2. It – the cat
3. He – the man
4. She – Laurie
5. it – the dish
6. She – Mum

B. 1. Laurie said, 'Okay, **I** will take the cat outside.'

2. The neighbours all said **they** had not lost a cat.

3. '**We** do not need that cat in our house,' said Mum.

4. Mum said, '**You** did well, Laurie, to find the cat's owner.'

5. The man was delighted when **he** saw the cat.

6. Laurie knew **she** brought too many stray animals home.

C. 1. it   3. you
2. me   4. him

D1. a. his   e. her
b. their   f. its
c. my   g. our
d. your

D2. her face *becomes* his face;
your lucky stars *becomes* my lucky stars;
their Tiger *becomes* my Tiger

4. Work on your … adjectives

A. 1. magic, last, beautiful, sunny, good

2. old, lush, green, little, great

3. narrow, winding, rocky, wide, fantastic

B. 1. small
2. huge
3. plenty
4. wide
5. gnarly
6. narrow

C. 1. d
2. a
3. f
4. e
5. b
6. c

D.

Adjective	Comparative	Superlative
beautiful	more beautiful	most beautiful
old	older	oldest
great	greater	greatest
winding	more winding	most winding
deep	deeper	deepest
special	more special	most special
awesome	more awesome	most awesome
gnarly	gnarlier	gnarliest
fantastic	more fantastic	most fantastic
bumpy	bumpier	bumpiest

E. 1. worse
2. least
3. worst
4. best
5. more
6. most
7. better
8. less

5. Work on your … verbs

A1. a. cycles
b. has
c. can get
d. can slip
e. are stuck
f. can use
g. takes
h. likes
i. pedals

A2. t. c
u. g
v. e
w. f
x. i
y. a
z. b

B. 1. d, h

2. a, i

3. g, j

4. f, k

5. c, l

6. b, e

C. 1. like   3. like   5. are
2. is   4. am   6. likes

D. 1. pedals (or goes)   4. works
2. looked   5. thought
3. went   6. will think

6. Work on your ... adverbs

A1. a. honestly, loudly   d. only
b. usually   e. *no adverb*
c. actually   f. suddenly

A2. Ask someone else to check your new sentences to see if they make sense.

B1. dramatically *adds* -ally;
easily *drops* -y *and adds* -ily;
fully *adds just* -y.

B2. a. really   c. eagerly   e. easily
b. lately   d. quickly   f. quietly

C.   1. partly *to* fully

       2. carefully *to* roughly

       3. quickly *to* slowly

       4. tensely *to* easily

       5. loudly *to* quietly

       6. wrongly *to* rightly

D.   1. c   3. b
       2. d   4. a

7. Work on your ... prepositions and conjunctions

A.   1. in   3. at   5. after
       2. from   4. into   6. with

B.   1. because 3. while   5. yet (*or* but)
       2. or   4. but (*or* yet) 6. so

C.   Various answers are correct. Ask someone else to check that the conjunction you chose for each sentence makes sense.

D.   1. at   6. and
       2. in   7. from
       3. on   8. by
       4. beside   9. but
       5. across   10. because

8. Revise your ... parts of speech

A. 1. weekends   4. parents
2. computer   5. Christmas
3. Mo   6. Josh

B. *Concrete:* Mo, computer, body

Abstract: weekends, holidays, minute

C. This chart for Question 2 includes the pronouns you should have circled in answer to Question 1 – they are the words in *italics*.

		Singular	**Plural**
1st person	Subject	*I*	we
	Object	*me*	us
	Possessive	*my*	our
2nd person	Subject	*you*	you
	Object	you	you
	Possessive	*your*	your
3rd person	Subject	*he, she,* it	*they*
	Object	him, her, *it*	*them*
	Possessive	*his, her* (or hers), its	*their*

D. 1. e   3. a   5. b
2. d   4. f   6. c

E. 1. plays (*links with* to play)

2. was (*links with* to be)

3. knew (*links with* to know)

4. use (*links with* to use)

5. enjoyed (*links with* to enjoy)

6. has (*links with* to have)

7. spent (*links with* to spend)

8. learnt (*links with* to learn)

F. really, gradually, easily, happily, technically, successfully, actually, already

(continued)

8. Revise your ... parts of speech (continued)

G. 1. on   3. at   5. for
2. about   4. in   6. to

H. 1. so   6. when
2. before   7. then
3. but   8. yet
4. and   9. after (*or* when)
5. because 10. until

I. Mo began to think that he would like to invent his own game. He knew what he liked and what he didn't like about different games. He thought he knew what would work better and what sort of setting would make a game more interesting.